Don't Sing at the Table

Don't Sing at the Table

(And Other Counsel from Grandma)

by

Shirley McCulloch

The quilt on the cover was made by the author's
great-grandmother, Ida J. Lindback.
It was photographed by Steve Bardolph, Jr.

The front cover drawing was made by
granddaughter Stephanie Kinney.

Bible quotes taken from the
New American Standard translation.

ISBN: 0-9714295-0-2

Pre-press by North Star Press of St. Cloud, Inc., St. Cloud,
Minnesota

Printing by Versa Press, Inc., East Peoria, Illinois.

Published by
SNB Publishing
13011 Deborah Lane SW
Motley, Minnesota 56466

FOR OUR GRANDCHILDREN, THOSE WHO
ARE ALREADY COPING WITH THE WORLD,
AND THOSE WHO HAVEN'T ARRIVED YET.

Acknowledgments

Thanks to my dear friend Rebecca Smith, who used her gift of exhortation to get me started, and to her husband Don, who told me I didn't have to write 366 pages, that I could quit when I didn't have any more to say.

Don't Sing at the Table

GRANDCHILDREN ARE THE CROWN OF OLD MEN, AND THE GLORY OF SONS IS THEIR FATHERS. (Proverbs 17:6)

Your grandpa Bud has encouraged me for the last ten years to do this book, and since he has a lot of influence on most of us, he deserves to be recognized. His views are quite often unorthodox, with speech patterns that confuse and confound. His role model and undisputed leader is Jesus. *The Little Engine that Could* probably comes in second.

I want to make sure you have the benefit of a few of his tenets that your parents learned years ago:

> The Crow Wing River is the true source of the Mississippi.

> Exercise is worthless if it doesn't result in a product such as a stack of wood, or maybe a house.

> Girls should know how to fix their cars, and guys should know how to bake bread, just in case.

> Horsepower is horsepower.

> There is no excuse for not answering your telephone. Your time is no more valuable than that of the person who is calling.

> Don't bother with a doctor unless something is bleeding badly or dangling by a thread.

> Read the Bible to correct yourself, not other people.

TRAIN UP A CHILD IN THE WAY HE SHOULD GO, EVEN WHEN HE IS OLD HE WILL NOT DEPART FROM IT. (Proverbs 22:6)

A few years ago I was startled by an article in the *Minneapolis Star Tribune*. Someone had conducted a study of all Minnesota's counties to determine the quality of life in each. Norman County was rated the lowest in the state. I remain curious about the criteria, and I can say with conviction that the quality of life for me in Norman County was great.

Norman County was the one place where I could count on unconditional love and security. It taught me several little lessons I carry to this day:

1. Never make fun of people for things they can't help, only things they CAN help. (Grandma Thompson had skinny legs, and endured much teasing when she was young.)

2. If the door opens and there's no one there, Aven Beinlaus just came in.

3. This day will never come again. (Grandma Lindback pointed that out to me one Sunday afternoon when I was four and bored.).

4. Don't sing at the table.

5. Try not to be an *utabuk* (closest translation "airhead").

6. People were meant to be awake when the sun is up and sleeping when it's down.

7. You're never too young to drink coffee, especially if you have just a little swig. (This was from Grandpa Thompson, who also believed that kids were just extremely short adults and should be spoken to that way.)

8. Cream and bread make an excellent breakfast. Milk dumplings are for supper. (I'll not belabor lutefisk and lefse. They've been done.)

9. It's important to be *decent.*

10. There's a lot of difference between a Norwegian and a Swede. (I'm still unclear on this.)

And the list goes on and on in my head. Thank you, Lord, for Norman County.

MY PRESENCE SHALL GO WITH YOU, AND I WILL GIVE YOU REST. (Exodus 33:14)

In 1990 we sold our home, used the money to buy a travel trailer and truck, and went out to serve because Bud heard the call to go. I wasn't nearly so sure his hearing was good, but I couldn't deny that he had considerable talent and expertise to share.

We went several places. The one that had the most life-changing effect on me was the time spent with the Tohono O'Odham. Some people know them as the Papago tribe. Their name means Desert People in English, and that they are.

As Anglos we have a terrible habit of thinking we know what's best for everyone else. We don't seem to know how to say, "What can I do for you?" and then listen for an answer. The O'odham are patient almost beyond belief with this annoying trait in us.

Once we relaxed and listened for what they wanted and then tried to honor that, we entered into a loving family, willing to share deep hurts and concerns, willing to share their humor, willing to teach us about their culture.

Don't let anyone tell you that television and the Internet have totally homogenized this country. Cultural differences are still with us. Stepping on cultural sensitivities is deadly to a ministry, and you may not even know you've done it.

We're not good listeners in most situations. That was probably lesson number one.

YOU HYPOCRITE, FIRST TAKE THE LOG OUT OF YOUR OWN EYE, AND THEN YOU WILL SEE CLEARLY TO TAKE THE SPECK OUT OF YOUR BROTHER'S EYE. (Matthew 7:5)

O'odham lesson # 2: They used the phrase "our way" often enough to catch my attention. After living among them for more than three years, I had observed quite a few differences between their way and ours, but it wasn't until I had an experience in our own little Presbyterian church at home that I learned my lesson.

A new leader came to our church, determined to change the way we worshiped. We weren't lively enough; we didn't wave our arms in the air. I was terribly uncomfortable but felt chastised and guilty. I began to grow angry and frustrated because I felt judged and prodded to do things that seemed against my nature. This person had no way of knowing if my worship was acceptable to God. I was truly struggling with the idea that I was "frozen." I would emerge from worship tense and almost bewildered by conflicting emotions.

Suddenly I remembered the O'odham, who could teach Anglo main-line church members everywhere lessons in how to be quiet. Everything fell into place in an instant. No more guilt. No more anger.

I now knew in a very small way what Native Americans have been tolerating for years from mission workers. I now knew why they would sometimes just look serenely at me and say, "It's not our way."

Lively worship is wonderful for those who are comfortable with it. It's just not "my way."

THUS SAYS THE LORD, "STAND BY THE WAYS AND SEE AND ASK FOR THE ANCIENT PATHS, WHERE THE GOOD WAY IS AND WALK IN IT." (Jeremiah 6:16)

We had been on the reservation just a few months when an older O'odham man knocked on the door and told me he had something to say. He was angry about many things going on at the church, especially at one group of volunteers who had worked on the church kitchen. Although he was not accurate in many of the accusations he made, and his confrontational approach is rather unusual there, he said something that kept me thinking for years afterward.

He said, "The trouble with you Anglos is you think in a straight line. It's always move ahead! Move ahead! Indians don't think in a straight line. They think in a circle."

I could see the truth in that as the years went by, and we saw for ourselves the respect for old people, old stories, old medicines, and the past in general. I began to wonder what the Bible had to say about that.

There's much in scripture that could be called circular thinking: "whoever wishes to save his life shall lose it" or "Many who are first will be last." Jesus' debates with the Pharisees are full of circular thinking.

Of course there is also straight-line thinking: "Forgetting what lies behind and reaching forward to what lies ahead . . ."

God won't be entrapped in any culture. Keep your mind open and look for the good way.

OLDER WOMEN LIKEWISE ARE TO BE REVERENT IN THEIR BEHAVIOR, NOT MALICIOUS GOSSIPS, NOR ENSLAVED TO MUCH WINE, TEACHING WHAT IS GOOD. (Titus 2:3)

This is good advice for old women. The evils of malicious gossip and too much wine are pretty obvious. It's the teaching part that is problematic to me.

There are still some cultures that honor and even revere the wisdom of their old. The Native American tribes seem to do that. I saw more honoring of older people among the Tohono O'odham than I have ever seen anywhere else. I have to wonder, though, if they aren't also in danger of losing that part of their way of life.

Old people are certainly not perceived as teachers in our society. They are has-beens who can't keep up. They are annoyances. I saw a bumper sticker in Phoenix: WHEN I RETIRE, I'M GOING TO MOVE TO MINNESOTA AND DRIVE REAL SLOW.

Another one said, SO MANY SNOWBIRDS, SO LITTLE FREEZER SPACE.

Yes, humorous, but also troubling. We've lost something. We've lost what Paul is talking about in this verse.

AND THERE WAS A CERTAIN YOUNG MAN
NAMED EUTYCHUS SITTING ON THE WINDOW
SILL, SINKING INTO A DEEP SLEEP; AND AS PAUL
KEPT ON TALKING, HE WAS OVERCOME BY SLEEP
AND FELL DOWN FROM THE THIRD FLOOR, AND
WAS PICKED UP DEAD. (Acts 20:9)

I heard a pastor say that if all the people in all the churches who fall asleep during the sermon were laid end to end, they would be a lot more comfortable.

Paul felt an urgency to get it all said because he had to leave the next day, but reality is that people will only listen for so long. If you are tuned to your listeners, you should be able to tell when you no longer have their attention.

Several years ago a speaker put on an incredible performance at a Bible camp meeting for junior high students. The night was warm and sticky, making a ten-minute talk about the limit. This man went on and on for an hour and a half with the kids becoming noisier and more wiggly with every miserable moment. The people in charge of the meeting didn't seem to know what to do.

Finally, the camp medic, suffering from a leg injury, made the long walk down the aisle on his crutches, one lurch at a time. When he finally reached the front, he said, "You have to stop."

Incredibly, the speaker protested with, "But I have just a few more things to say."

"You have to stop."

What possible good can come from talking when there are no listeners?

MY SHEEP HEAR MY VOICE AND I KNOW THEM, AND THEY FOLLOW ME. (John 10:27)

How can all the people in all the Christian denominations across the world be so sure they're right and everyone else is wrong? Don't we all follow Jesus?

Yes we do, and no we don't.

Mostly, no we don't. We don't because our own imaginations get in the way. We invent Him in our minds. Some days my Jesus disapproves of the same people I do. He is in total accord with all my opinions. He is angry at the very same people I'm angry with, and He makes excuses for all my behavior. It's very comfortable. It's also slippery spiritual ground.

Think about your Jesus. If He agrees with you on baptism, communion, the inerrancy of scripture, abortion, capital punishment, political parties, and so on, you've stepped out ahead of Him somewhere. You're leading Him, not following, and the distance between you and Him is becoming greater and greater.

You'd better turn around and find your way back. He never told us to lead Him. He said we should follow.

FOR MY THOUGHTS ARE NOT YOUR THOUGHTS. NEITHER ARE MY WAYS YOUR WAYS. (Isaiah 55: 7-8)

Why is regular Bible study so important? Why can't we simply rely on God to speak to us through the Holy Spirit when we're praying?

Because we're human, and it's too easy to rationalize and fool ourselves. We have a tendency to create God in terms of our own temperament: "I think this way. It's a reasonable way to think; therefore, God must think this way too." We create a God similar to cartoon Calvin's Hobbes.

God doesn't like that. Constantly going to the scriptures and giving Him the chance to reveal Himself to us there is our best insurance against fooling ourselves.

AND THE LORD SAID TO SATAN, "FROM WHERE DO YOU COME?" THEN SATAN ANSWERED THE LORD AND SAID, "FROM ROAMING ABOUT ON THE EARTH AND WALKING AROUND ON IT."

(Job 1:7)

Billy Graham was being interviewed by David Frost on PBS. He said he believes the earth is the only planet God has allowed Satan to rule. I hope he's right. He's made enough of a mess here.

Does talk about Satan and demons make you uncomfortable? Are you part of the "rational" reasoning of the world that pooh-poohs Satan's existence? If you are a Christian, you cannot pooh-pooh it. Jesus took Satan very seriously. Either you believe Jesus, or you don't.

Remember that evil is real. Pray for growth in understanding of what is good, and ask for discernment to recognize evil. Often evil seems harmless and ordinary.

DO YOU BELIEVE IN THE SON OF MAN?
(John 9: 35 RSV)

Jesus often asked questions. His questions have always intrigued me because He obviously already knew the answers.

There seems to be a pattern, some broad categories the questions fall into. There are the "Know ye not?" questions, containing some reference to scripture. There are the lawyer-like questions that he used in confrontations. Then there were the questions like the one above, seemingly designed to make us think about our own spiritual condition.

Does Jesus have credibility with you, or do you pick and choose what you want from His words? To be His total child, you must be totally open to all His words.

JESUS SAID TO HER, DID I NOT TELL YOU THAT IF YOU WOULD BELIEVE YOU WOULD SEE THE GLORY OF GOD? (John 11:40)

"I'll have to see that to believe it." "Seeing is believing." "You'll have to show me that before I'll believe it."

In our world, a certain amount of cynicism is considered healthy and reasonable.

That isn't what Jesus said. He did not say, "Seeing is believing." He said that believing is seeing. Does that mean if I don't believe, he won't show me anything?

Probably.

BUT GROW IN THE GRACE AND KNOWLEDGE OF OUR LORD AND SAVIOR JESUS CHRIST. (2 Peter 3:18)

This verse assigns to us what may be the most important duty that we have. It is a command. In grammatical terms, this is called the imperative mode. In Greek, the command would have been very clear. In English we spell the word "grow" the same way whether it's a command or not, so some of the punch is lost. This is unfortunate because it's very important.

We have orders to become better acquainted with Christ. Our main priority and responsibility is to mature. The things we must work on are called the fruit of the Spirit. (Galations 5:22)

Do you know Him better than you did a year ago? Well, get at it and grow!! Imperative mode.

IT IS MORE BLESSED TO GIVE THAN TO RECEIVE.
(Acts 20:35)

I once knew a woman who talked much about the gifts she had given and what she had done for others. As gestures of friendship, I would bring her gifts from time to time. I was always left with an odd, empty feeling. She was not gracious and definitely made me feel uncomfortable. At the time I thought, "Well, I guess she's just better at giving than at receiving."

I now realize that she wasn't good at giving either. She was chronically angry at someone who hadn't said "thank-you" or had neglected her in some way. She complained constantly about not being appreciated.

Jesus knew how to give. He gave of His time, His special powers, His knowledge, and, finally, He gave Himself. But He also knew how to receive. He accepted hospitality from many different kinds of people, and He accepted gifts. (John 12:3 and Luke 8:3)

Pray that you will lose your sense of self in both giving and receiving, for they are tied together. If you don't know how to show love when you're receiving, you don't know how to give either. The two are not really separable.

THE SPIRIT OF THE LORD IS UPON ME, BECAUSE HE HAS ANNOINTED ME TO PREACH THE GOSPEL TO THE POOR . . . TO PROCLAIM THE FAVORABLE YEAR OF THE LORD . . . AND HE CLOSED THE BOOK . . . (Luke 4:18-20)

The way Jesus chose to launch His ministry is extremely significant and is not talked about very much. First, there was the temptation in the wilderness, from which he emerged with His plan. Then there was this incident in the Nazareth synagogue.

A rabbi would take the scroll he wanted and read from it, emphasizing and teaching as he went. Jesus chose Isaiah 61, a favorite because it was known to contain assurance that the Jews would prevail in the Day of the Lord.

He read about preaching the gospel, proclaiming release to the captives, freeing the downtrodden, etc.; but just as he reached everyone's favorite part, the part about the Jewish Day of the Lord and His vengeance, He stopped without reading it and closed the book.

We must focus on God's will so we don't focus only on our own favorite places. God's vengeance and judgment were not Jesus' priorities this time around, and they're not ours either.

FORGETTING WHAT LIES BEHIND AND REACH-
ING FORWARD TO WHAT LIES AHEAD, I PRESS ON
TOWARD THE GOAL FOR THE PRIZE OF THE
UPWARD CALL OF GOD IN CHRIST JESUS.

(Philippians 3:13-14)

If you've ever heard a sermon on this passage, it probably
was full of athletic analogies with examples of endurance, persist-
ence, and, finally, winning the trophy.

There's something else, almost hidden in this passage,
though, that is just as important. If I am thinking about what happened in the past, some failure or frustration, I'm not giving the correct attention to what I should be doing right now.

Pray for the will to forget what lies behind so yesterday can't
cripple today for you.

HAD TWO SONS, AND HE CAME TO THE FIRST, AND SAID, "SON, GO WORK IN THE VINEYARD." (Matthew 21:28)

This story reminds me of my brother Rich and our somewhat rocky relationship when we were kids. When the father told the first son to work in the vineyard, he said he would go, and then he did not. When the father told the second son to go, he rebelliously said he would not go. He soon regretted his answer, changed his mind, and went to do his father's work.

Rich would always take the path of most resistance and then end up doing the right thing because he had a good heart and was utterly dependable. This path, however, led to more confrontations with Dad than I had. I found it easier to say I agreed and then go ahead with my own agenda on the chance that Dad would forget. This bought me long periods of time when I didn't have to work in the vineyard.

However, Dad eventually figured it out, as I'm sure the father in the parable did. Jesus stated quite dramatically that He preferred the second son to the first. When we're called to serve, we must not promise if we don't intend to keep the promise.

LOVE IS PATIENT, LOVE IS KIND . . . DOES NOT ACT UNBECOMINGLY; IT DOES NOT SEEK ITS OWN.
(1 Corinthians 13: 4,5)

The scary thing about being a role model is that we usually are not aware that it's happening. I'm sure my mother consciously tried to model many traits and values for me and my brothers. In some things she succeeded, and I'm fairly sure she considered herself a failure in others.

When my grandfather died, she was so focused on her mother that I know she wasn't thinking about role modeling. The way she handled the situation left a powerful impression on me.

Grandma wanted two funerals for him. I was in my early thirties, which meant, of course, that I knew everything. My knee-jerk reaction was to shout, "Are you wacky? Twin Valley is 200 miles from here. Pick one place, and let's get on with it!!!"

My mother calmly said, "Whatever you want. This is your decision."

She spent the rest of the day asking Grandma what she wanted in detail and carrying it all out. Her patience and servant-like attitude humbled me because I was sure she had opinions similar to mine about some of the choices.

Listening to her, I made up my mind that when the time came, I would try to be as patient and cooperative as she had been. I'm a little rougher around the edges than she, but her example was strong enough when she passed away and we had to help our dad through it.

FOR OF HIS FULLNESS WE HAVE ALL RECEIVED, AND GRACE UPON GRACE. (John 1:16)

Which is more difficult for you? When someone actually does something to hurt you, or when you have the abandoned feeling that the person failed you by not doing something? The first requires forgiveness. The second requires pure grace.

Growing in grace is a life-long struggle for most of us. We may master little matters such as letting someone go ahead of us in the supermarket line, but we defend our bad attitudes in other situations. We make up our minds before we really know anything. We find fault. We harbor resentment, and we fertilize it. This never feels good.

Grace is crucial. Forgiveness must be accompanied by grace. We forgive someone for a specific reason and then we forget it. Forgetting is the grace.

Grace is a revelation when you opt for it. You will be very pleasantly surprised at how much easier life is without all those uncomfortable resentments. We forgive for a specific reason. We can extend grace for no reason.

At first you will have to make a special effort to think about grace and show grace. After a while it will ease your load, become part of you. You will feel freer than you ever have before.

LET JUSTICE ROLL DOWN LIKE WATERS AND RIGHT-EOUSNESS LIKE AN EVER-FLOWING STREAM.
(Amos 5:24)

There are many people in this world who have been willing to stand up for what was right even if it meant going to prison. I have had the privilege of knowing only two personally. One of them is John Fife. He is pastor at Southside Presbyterian Church in Tucson, Arizona.

In the 1980s he and his congregation went through the turmoil of what became known as the Sanctuary Movement. People from Latin America were appealing to them for help in order to escape the death squads. He was willing to go to prison rather than ignore what he knew God was telling him to do.

John probably doesn't know it, but he taught me something very important about what serving really is. According to him, doing social good isn't worth much if you don't move into relationship with the people you're serving. It isn't good enough to work in a soup kitchen. You have to develop a relationship with the people eating the soup.

Jesus did that. The Pharisees couldn't understand his friendships with the unclean. They could see that he insisted on a relationship with those to whom he ministered, but they chose not to understand it.

Whether we are serving soup, building houses, giving shelter, giving handouts, or giving Bible studies, we should be seeing Jesus' face in the faces of the poor. And they had better be able to see His in ours. Where else are they going to see Him?

John taught me the essential steps. When you move into relationship, you begin to care about them. You want life to be better for them, so you work for justice.

UNLESS THE LORD BUILDS THE HOUSE, THEY LABOR IN VAIN WHO BUILD IT. Psalm 127: 1

Toward the end of his life, Grandpa Milt began to take inventory. He was a person who had been much honored and recognized for public service during his working years. I remember attending many open houses and dinners in his honor over the years. There is a library named after him.

I had been helping him write his memoirs for a few years, but after he died, I found some I hadn't seen before. His one regret was that he hadn't taken enough time to make sure the Lord was building the house.

I know he understood that his salvation was in Jesus, that God oversees and has sovereignty. But I don't think he saw until it was almost too late that God also leads if you seek guidance.

If we don't realize that and take advantage of it, we miss out on so much. We miss out on the everyday personal relationship. We miss out on the wise counsel. We miss out on the peace of mind. We miss out on the richer life here on earth.

He wanted us to think about that.

THE ANGEL OF THE LORD ENCAMPS AROUND THOSE WHO FEAR HIM, AND RESCUES THEM.
Psalm 34:7

Have you ever been afraid? Being an instinctive fretter, I, of course, have been afraid many times.

Living on the southern side of Tucson for a while was probably the only time I've actually been in danger. We could hear gunshots almost every night and watch drug deals being made in the alley. Living in an RV with its thin walls was unnerving.

It's almost impossible to grasp that countless people in this world have to live in fear all of the time.

I remember another time, many years ago, when I was afraid. A friend gave me this verse and told me to claim it. I did.

I'm leaving it with you for a time when you may need it.

HE . . . SAID, "LOOK! I SEE FOUR MEN LOOSED AND WALKING ABOUT IN THE MIDST OF THE FIRE WITHOUT HARM, AND THE APPEARANCE OF THE FOURTH IS LIKE A SON OF THE GODS!"

(Daniel 3:25)

The book of Daniel is filled with amazing, miraculous events. This story of the three young men thrown into Nebuchadnezzar's furnace is a wonderful illustration of freedom in bondage and extremely strong faith.

Most of us have never been tested in a way that puts our lives in peril. I suppose most of us dread that because we don't know for sure that we would have enough courage and faith. I can promise that your faith will be tested. I cannot promise that you will express your faith as forcefully as these young men did. That would be your choice.

Neither can I promise that you will always feel your faith has been vindicated. When you don't think it is being vindicated, you're still being tested.

One thing is for sure. There is freedom in the certainty of your faith. The more steadfast your faith, the less tied up you are. It's the peace that Jesus talks about in the book of John when he says his peace isn't like any peace the world gives.

THE WALL FELL DOWN FLAT . . . (Joshua 6:20)

It's hard to imagine the insecurities the Israelites must have felt when they reached Canaan. They had known only nomadic life for so many years under the very strong leadership of Moses. They had been given food to eat and had been led by a pillar of cloud and fire from God.

Moses was dead, and Joshua was to lead them. I remember my mother talking about how she felt when President Franklin Roosevelt died. He was the only president she had ever known, and she said it was very frightening to her.

Also there was no pillar of cloud anymore, and the manna had ceased. They would have to live from the produce of the land, and they would have to pray for guidance. Those changes must have seemed huge to them.

You, too, will enter new plateaus in your life when you feel you've lost the security of the past and all you have is your faith. You will probably lose your parents; you may find yourself far away from home; familiar comforts may disappear on you. The possibilities are many.

If you read Chapters One to Eight of the book of Joshua, you will find a story of fumbling, defeat, and victory. When they failed, it was because they didn't seek and follow God's guidance. As God's children, we never do seem to get the hang of that consistently.

AND SHE SAID, "I WILL SURELY GO WITH YOU; NEVERTHELESS, THE HONOR SHALL NOT BE YOURS ON THE JOURNEY THAT YOU ARE ABOUT TO TAKE, FOR THE LORD WILL SELL SISERA INTO THE HANDS OF A WOMAN." (Judges 4:9)

Deborah was a judge. One can only speculate on the gender bias at the time. This verse indicates to me that there might have been some.

She had ordered a man named Barak to call up an army and subdue the leader of the Canaanite king's army. Barak said he would not go unless Deborah went with him.

She was obviously endowed with physical strength to be able to even consider such an undertaking. She was also shrewd enough to warn Barak that if she went, the glory would not be his because the Lord would be delivering Sisera into a woman's hands.

Great leaders must possess both physical strength and wisdom. Being a leader is tiring and requires stamina. One need only look at how much our presidents age during a four-year term to see that.

But what is physical ability without wisdom? It's Esau. It's Absalom. It's several basketball players I can think of who can jump, pass, shoot, and almost fly, but who don't think. They can't lead without wisdom.

Seek wisdom. It's a burden sometimes, but you can't do much without it.

BUT RUTH SAID, DO NOT URGE ME TO LEAVE YOU OR TURN BACK . . . FOR WHERE YOU GO, I WILL GO, AND WHERE YOU LODGE, I WILL LODGE. YOUR PEOPLE SHALL BE MY PEOPLE, AND YOUR GOD, MY GOD. (Ruth 1:16)

The commitment of this young woman to her mother-in-law is not explainable. A young woman recently said to me that she thinks God sometimes gifts us with extra grace toward a certain person when no one else understands why. I think she's right.

God also gifts us once in a while with unwavering loyalty and love from another person that seems to defy logic. Or we don't know what we did to prompt such devotion. Maybe we did nothing special. Maybe Naomi did nothing special. God just gave Ruth the love.

King David is a model of closeness to God. There was violence and disloyalty from his children. King Saul was a greatly flawed man. His children followed him to their own deaths. Who can explain it?

Have you offered such a commitment to anyone? Has anyone offered such a commitment to you? Are you open to it, or have you just tossed it away?

AT THAT TIME JESUS ANSWERED AND SAID, "I PRAISE THEE, O FATHER, LORD OF HEAVEN AND EARTH, THAT THOU DIDST HIDE THESE THINGS FROM THE WISE AND INTELLIGENT AND DIDST REVEAL THEM TO BABES." (Matthew 11:25)

The context of these words is not clear to me in Matthew. Luke (Chapter 10, Verse 21) helps a little. Jesus is clearly dealing with *babes*, people who don't understand much yet.

Condemning intellectuals and favoring non-intellectuals always fills me with trepidation. Ignorance is not a thing to be sought. So what is Jesus talking about here?

It is very clear in Luke 24:45 that the scriptures were to be studied. Being learned is not in itself a bad thing.

So, when does it become a bad thing? Probably when the wise and intelligent have closed minds. We can never learn so much that we're safe in turning off our eyes and ears. We will never have everything figured out.

If you've ever tried to communicate with a rebellious teenager, you know there's a big difference between enduring a speech and actually listening to it. Sometimes we listen. Sometimes we just sit. Sometimes we walk away.

The issue is openness. Children or *babes* are open. Jesus wants our hearts and our minds to be open. He will help us make correct judgments after we have listened. Not before.

Christians today, like the Pharisees, do a lot of judging before they listen. Remain open as much as you can. It won't hurt.

NOW DEBORAH, A PROPHETESS, THE WIFE OF
LAPPIDOTH, WAS JUDGING ISRAEL AT THAT
TIME. SHE USED TO SIT UNDER THE PALM TREE OF
DEBORAH . . . AND THE SONS OF ISRAEL CAME UP
TO HER FOR JUDGMENT. (Judges 4: 4,5)

This was a remarkable time in the history of the Israelites.
They had no king. Different judges ruled over different areas, and
they handled what we would call civil disputes. They were also mili-
tary leaders because there were Canaanites still living in the land.

The Israelites had strayed from the Lord's will again and
were being held by the king who reigned in Hazor. This is a pattern
that you will see over and over in the Old Testament: The people
stray; God brings them back by using the prophets.

God's grace.

We read about the Israelites. We read about the Pharisees.
We say, "What in the world was wrong with them? Why did they
disobey God? Why did they ignore God?"

Why do we?

NAKED I CAME FROM MY MOTHER'S WOMB, AND NAKED I SHALL RETURN THERE. THE LORD GAVE AND THE LORD HAS TAKEN AWAY. BLESSED BE THE NAME OF THE LORD. (Job 1:21)

Job had suffered great loss but was still holding firm in his faith in God. He had a long way to go because he hadn't yet been judged and tormented by his friends, who were sure they knew why this had happened to him.

The truth of this passage became totally real to me when my father was dying. A man of dignity and integrity brought low by a failing heart. He became dependent and helpless but never lost his courage and grace. A cousin summed him up when he said, "Milt is a gentleman."

But he was a gentleman alone. The solitary nature of our entry and exit from this world cannot be avoided.

This passage and its context are mainly about loss, though, not death. It gives a special perspective even if it may seem a bit dark. Job hadn't lost the things that are eternal, and the rest he wouldn't be keeping anyway.

Lying helpless in a hospital bed brings that truth home. It's best if you can learn it before that.

You will be a happier person and much closer to the Lord.

THEREFORE, CONFESS YOUR SINS TO ONE AN-OTHER, AND PRAY FOR ONE ANOTHER, SO THAT YOU MAY BE HEALED. (James 5:16)

This verse goes on to Elijah and how the prayer of a righteous man can accomplish much. My simple understanding of righteousness is that it means being right with God. Being in the right in God's eyes, not our own.

When we're right in our own eyes, we're self-righteous. Not good.

Self-righteousness and our other sins are supposed to be confessed to one another as well as to God. Interestingly, I don't think I've heard very much confessing to one another in our church families. Have you? I've heard a lot of complaining and criticising but not much confessing.

Confessing and clearing the way will aid our prayers and bring about the healing. It may be healing of physical bodies or of spirits.

Come to think of it, I haven't done very much confessing myself.

Healing is the goal.

SO YOU TOO, WHEN YOU DO ALL THE THINGS WHICH ARE COMMANDED YOU, SAY, "WE ARE UNWORTHY SLAVES: WE HAVE DONE ONLY THAT WHICH WE OUGHT TO HAVE DONE."

(Luke 17:10)

Americans are very proud and arrogant people when it comes to rights. Our whole government structure is built on rights. I have rights.

It's difficult, almost impossible, for us to think in terms of humility and obedience because "we have rights." We rankle at lectures about obedience.

I can't find any encouragement from Jesus to think that way. Nowhere does he tell me to exert my rights.

I suspect our country has been blessed, not because we have rights, but because we almost incidentally hit on the right thing by granting rights to others.

Many Christians don't grant others the right to be wrong or to think differently. When we quit respecting others, we will surely lose this blessing.

FOR ALL THESE THINGS THE NATIONS OF THE WORLD EAGERLY SEEK; BUT YOUR FATHER KNOWS THAT YOU NEED THESE THINGS. BUT SEEK FOR HIS KINGDOM AND THESE THINGS SHALL BE ADDED TO YOU. (Luke 12: 30-31)

There's another translation which says, "Seek first the kingdom of God and His righteousness and all these things will seek you."

I like the image that the things I need will actually come and find me if I am trying to be right with God.

We often fail at this because we invent in our own minds our own little God. He must think as we think. He becomes a larger version of ourselves, justifying all our opinions. That's not righteousness. It's self-righteousness.

The only way to be sure of what God thinks is to seek Him. Search the scriptures to learn to know Him better on virtually countless subjects. Seek him in prayer as Jesus did. Find your own lonely place.

You will never do well if you can't separate your own opinions and prejudices from what He really wants.

JESUS SAID TO HIM, "ARISE, TAKE UP YOUR PAL-LET, AND WALK." (John 5:8)

The man picked up his pallet and walked. He wanted help, and Jesus gave it to him.

When I read about the healings of Jesus, I think about the way most of us handle our giving. There's too much stinginess and control in most giving.

Doing our volunteer work for ten years has put us into contact with many personalities and many different motives. Rarely was the motive to give total help. It is almost always doled out in such a way that many receive a little help, but hardly anyone receives enough to get a real leg up.

Habitat for Humanity gives substantial help. There are some choices in each individual chapter that could probably stand some scrutiny, but mostly Habitat makes a noticeable change in circumstances.

If you listen to people talk about how they give and where they give, you will often hear pride at how many places they give money. The problem there is that many get a little and no one gets enough to make a difference.

What if Jesus had said, "Well, I'll heal one of your legs, but you might get too cocky if I fix both of them. Besides, I might need the energy later to fix one eye for somebody else."

Think about your giving, whether it's money or time. If you feel led to help someone, find a real way to help.

I WILL GIVE THANKS TO THEE, FOR I AM FEAR-FULLY AND WONDERFULLY MADE. (Psalm 139:14)

As I grow older and notice certain of my systems starting to fail, I still think about this passage. Maybe more so, because there's a consciousness of how the body used to work. Pretty amazing.

A few years ago, my dad said, "As my body grows older, the repair jobs come closer and closer together." I'm beginning to experience that truth now in ways that no one really wants to hear about.

Gene therapy and other medical breakthroughs will probably help, but there's one oddly comforting thought that comes to me once in a while as I struggle with menopausae, dental problems, and a growing inability to remember names. Maybe the deterioration of my body will make it emotionally easier to leave it.

Genetics and spirituality are going to have some interesting confrontations.

THE HEAVENS ARE TELLING OF THE GLORY OF
GOD; AND THEIR EXPANSE IS DECLARING THE
WORK OF HIS HANDS. DAY TO DAY POURS
FORTH SPEECH, AND NIGHT TO NIGHT REVEALS
KNOWLEDGE. THERE IS NO SPEECH, NOR ARE
THERE WORDS; THEIR VOICE IS NOT HEARD.

(Psalm 19: 1-3)

The McCullochs are mostly outdoor people. This passage
should be meaningful.

We don't always need words to learn. Sometimes God uses
words. Sometimes He doesn't. Power and glory are everywhere in
Creation. He has shown us so much of it, that Paul says God has
made His own power and nature so evident that we are "without
excuse." (Romans 1:20)

Nature isn't the only vehicle God uses to show us His power
and will. You will be given many opportunities to pick up on something without benefit of words. You will see pain and suffering and
need all around you. You will also see love, generosity, and grace dem-
onstrated in unexpected ways.

We all know intellectually our actions overpower our words,
and we're very good at picking up on the negative things people do.
We find it easy to point out hypocrisy all around us.

That's fine. There is hypocrisy, and we need to recognize it.
I'm not so sure we need to point it out, though. Better to look
around for a good example and emulate that than to jump up and
down about what's wrong.

He is showing us the way constantly. How receptive you are
to His subtle guidance is up to you.

FINALLY, BRETHREN, WHATEVER IS TRUE, WHATEVER IS HONORABLE, WHATEVER IS RIGHT, WHATEVER IS PURE, WHATEVER IS LOVELY, WHATEVER IS OF GOOD REPUTE, IF THERE IS ANY EXCELLENCE AND IF ANYTHING WORTHY OF PRAISE, LET YOUR MIND DWELL ON THESE THINGS. (Philippians 4:8)

In the American Standard translation this verse is in a section entitled "Peace with self." Having a sense of well-being, being at peace within, is not impossible. It need not come and go.

It is, however, a gift. It is a gift from God when we choose to accept it. It isn't a feeling. It's a whole way of being, and we choose it. This verse gives us a clear guide to dwelling in that place. We have been given minds to use as we wish.

Wouldn't it be wonderful if everyone in our homes and everyone in our church families would train their minds to concentrate on all of the above? What would happen to criticism, hurt, gossip, misunderstanding?

Sadly, we humans have developed such unhealthy ways of thinking, that concentrating on these things seems impossible. It is not impossible.

Try this: Write the verse down and put it up somewhere where you will see it often. Try living it for a day. Two days. Keep going. When you slip, deliberately put your mind back on something that is true, honorable, worthy of praise, etc.

Paul says to practice. You'll enjoy it.

BE ANXIOUS FOR NOTHING, BUT IN EVERYTHING BY PRAYER AND SUPPLICATION WITH THANKS-GIVING LET YOUR REQUESTS BE MADE KNOWN TO GOD. (Philippians 4:6)

This imperative has so much in it that it's difficult to know where to start. The verse following it is the encouragement or exhortation.

First, we aren't supposed to worry about anything. About *anything*. Think about some circumstance that's bothering you right now. Worry is just another word for fear, so what little or big fear are you enslaved by today?

Your particular problem is the "everything" in the verse. In your specific problem you are to use thanks and pleas for help. It seems to be telling us to "spell out" exactly what is bothering us and maybe even to say what we want to happen.

The giving of thanks is not a bribe. It puts us in true communion with Him. And because God is not limited to one concept of time as we are, the thanksgiving shows our confidence that He is sovereign and has the problem under control.

Verse Seven goes on to say that if we do this, a unique peace will follow, a peace that guards our hearts and our minds. A guarded heart and a guarded mind will not be so vulnerable to worry next time.

BLESS THE LORD, O MY SOUL; AND ALL THAT IS WITHIN ME BLESS HIS HOLY NAME. BLESS THE LORD, O MY SOUL, AND FORGET NONE OF HIS BENEFITS. (Psalm 103: 1,2)

There is something in my Scandinavian being that does not take easily to praise. I don't expect it. I don't give it or take it very naturally. That's wrong.

God tells us to praise Him, and a whole new world will open up for us. There is something energizing about counting blessings. If I take time to recount some ways that God has blessed me, what I should be grateful for, I'm always comforted when I realize how many benefits there are.

Sometimes I have found myself saying, "Why me, Lord? Why have I been so richly blessed?" There is no answer for that, but it's a refreshing change from asking the same question about my problems.

Exuberant, jumping-up-and-down praise is quite popular now. I still don't quite have the hang of that, but there is a strong confidence and strength that comes from naming God's benefits in prayer and praise.

You don't have to shout and wave your arms. You can do it quietly. Just do it.

SEE HOW GREAT A LOVE THE FATHER HAS BESTOWED UPON US THAT WE SHOULD BE CALLED CHILDREN OF GOD; AND SUCH WE ARE.
(1 John 3:1)

Grammar may be incomprehensible and tedious to many people, but it is worth noting from time to time. This is a wonderful passage of comfort.

The Father "has bestowed" love. It's a past action. He gave us the love. It's expressed in the present perfect tense, which means it started in the past but continues into the present. It's ongoing.

Many people are consumed with the future. We know Jesus told us not to do that, but we do it anyway. This focus on what's going to happen spills over into our concepts about Christ's Kingdom. We think of it as something that will occur someday, not something that has already begun.

This passage says we "are" the children of God. Present tense. Now. It doesn't say we will be His children at some future time.

Think how astounding this must have been for people living in the first century. Most of the Jews probably thought of themselves as Abraham's children, but to be God's child would be a stretch. The Canaanites who sacrificed their babies and worshipped other gods certainly thought of themselves more as subjects or slaves than as children.

He gave us the love in the past, and He continues it. You are a child of the Kingdom, and you can live in it now.

AND SUCH WE ARE.

AND HE WILL BE LIKE A TREE FIRMLY PLANTED BY
STREAMS OF WATER, WHICH YIELDS ITS FRUIT IN
ITS SEASON, AND ITS LEAF DOES NOT WITHER.

Psalm 1:3

This is a most beautiful reassurance for me as I grow older. It speaks to my concept of ministry. Every believer is meant to have one, I think. That's why it is so helpful to think about your spiritual gifts. God has fit us for His service. In what way are you gifted to minister to others?

As we have lived in retirement parks in the southwest, we have seen something very sad. People seem to fall into two basic categories in these places. The first are those who still have pretty good health and spend most of their day working very hard at having fun. It's important to "stay busy," you know.

The second group have lost most of their health and mobility. They just sit.

This verse tells me that no matter what age I am, I still have a ministry. As long as I have my "marbles," even if I'm not in very good physical health, I will still be firmly planted and will still have use. I won't wither in ministry or spirit.

Is your busyness a ministry, or is it just busyness?

FOR MY YOKE IS EASY, AND MY LOAD IS LIGHT.
(Matthew 11:30)

When you decide to become a believer, you are dealing with your own eternal security. When you decide that you wish to learn about Jesus and to follow him, you put on the "yoke" and become his disciple. You are now dealing with how you're going to live your life here on earth.

Jesus was involved in many confrontations with church leaders. Their rules for daily living were impossible for the average person to follow because there were so many. God laid out many rules and guidelines in the Old Testament, and Jewish leaders expanded on those to an unbearable extreme. Only those who devoted their lives to studying all the laws were sure they were righteous.

Along came Jesus introducing grace.

We've heard His message so many times that we may not realize how difficult and frustrating it must have been for those who felt they tried hard to follow the rules but were never quite making it. The Pharisees were always there to point out the failings.

There are Christian Pharisees too. They want all the I's dotted and T's crossed in just the correct way. Don't let them intimidate you. You're a follower of Jesus and His way. He wants your mind freed so you will listen to what He wants you to do.

Remember grace.

I SET MY BOW IN THE CLOUD, AND IT SHALL BE FOR A SIGN OF A COVENANT BETWEEN ME AND THE EARTH. (Genesis 9:13)

We all enjoy a rainbow. It's a reminder that God is still there, keeping promises.

And it's beautiful.

It's also a reminder that we *are without excuse* if we fail to see evidence of God's existence in all creation. (Romans 1:20)

Now, I'm not exactly an "out-doorsey" person. I have a two-degree comfort range, seventy to seventy-two. My idea of a good dewpoint is seven. Despite this, God's creation has made itself known to me.

Our family has been blessed by the beautiful north woods and lakes. The Navajo and Tohono O'odham reservations bear witness to God's power and creativity. I can enjoy and appreciate the beauty even if I don't want to be out in it much.

I don't even have to go find the birds. They come to me.

If you're living in a city with all the hurry, concrete, fumes, and road rage, it's probably necessary to get to some trees and green grass so you're not cannibalized. Or, if you're living in the desert, forget the green grass. The desert has its own beauty and has been healing for me.

And even in the desert we have the rainbow. After the storm, the wind and the terrifying lightning, there it is.

Renewal and hope.

FOR I AM MINDFUL OF THE SINCERE FAITH WITH-IN YOU, WHICH FIRST DWELT IN YOUR GRAND-MOTHER LOIS, AND YOUR MOTHER EUNICE, AND I AM SURE THAT IT IS IN YOU AS WELL. (2 Timothy 1:5)

We know we can't inherit salvation or even faith, but if you were fortunate enough to have parents or grandparents of faith, you have a head start on getting your life going right. You already know where the good way is that Jeremiah talks about. (Jer. 6:16)

You will be granted a certain amount of credibility based on who your parents or grandparents were. That's what Paul is doing here with Timothy.

However, that grace will not last forever. You will have to come to belief and claim it for your own.

Even during that period of decision you have a powerful blessing. Those parents and grandparents are praying for you. When you're young, if you're rebelling or struggling with faith, that may seem like an annoyance or a burden. But let me tell you, there's no one more tenacious than a praying grandmother. She's not going to quit, and she will pray with an objectivity and absence of fear for you.

If you have a grandmother who is praying for you, you may as well give up and pay attention to what the Lord wants. You're going to eventually.

NOT THAT I SPEAK FROM WANT, FOR I HAVE LEARNED TO BE CONTENT IN WHATEVER CIRCUMSTANCES I AM. (Philippians 4:11)

Paul seems to be a Type-A or choleric personality. His statement is remarkable since that temperament type is hardly ever content. They want projects and constant action.

Contentment really isn't part of the American psyche at all. When we meet a person who seems content, most of us probably wonder what's wrong with him or her. We throw around terms like *unmotivated* or even *lazy*.

We think about achievement. We want our children to be goal oriented. As my son Sean said to me, "When you're talking about what you want for me, you take on a choleric persona." I answered, "Well, I'm your mother. That's my job."

Paul talks about his circumstances. The world throws all kinds of circumstances at us. Some of them are pretty difficult. As a great-aunt of mine said to me when I was about twelve, "You've had a good life. But you wait. Something terrible will happen." Eventually, a few things did happen, of course.

Paul was in prison when he wrote Philippians. That's the great thing about contentment. It's not a goal. It's a choice.

THEN THE LORD ANSWERED JOB OUT OF THE WHIRLWIND. Job 38:1

I love this verse. It's powerful and beautiful and creates for us an image of a God at the end of patience.

I'm not sure if it has any practical application for me right now except as a reminder that God probably gets tired of our constant talking and our failure to grant Him the same grace that He has granted us.

We say, "How can God allow such a thing?" or "I just don't know why God is letting this happen to me." My personal favorite was a woman who said she just didn't understand why God didn't want her to have a dining room. He couldn't possibly be denying her that basic human right, could he?

We must be so very irritating at times with our self-pity and whining.

Be grateful when He speaks to you in a small, still voice. Try not to provoke Him to speaking to you out of the whirlwind. It will be much less pleasant.

DO NOT FRET. IT LEADS ONLY TO EVILDOING.
Psalm 37:8

I'm one of the all-time great fretters. I often make a perfectly workable plan and then spend the next few hours convincing myself that it won't work because this could go wrong, or that could go wrong.

Or I wake up in the night and start fretting about past wrongs done to me or by me, about my children and grandchildren, about the stock market, about whether we're out of paper towels. Whatever.

If fretting were merely a waste of time and energy, I wouldn't mention it here. As this verse says, it's more ominous than that.

If I'm angry at someone, the anger builds. If I'm worrying about something, my paranoia grows. I can emphatically say I have never solved a problem when I was fretting. What I have done is let the fretting lead me to some very bad decisions.

But how do I stop fretting when it seems so ingrained? Praying is the only antidote. I try to lay out the problem in a very logical, orderly way for the Lord. I think of Him as smiling at this, but I do it anyway. It's therapy for me. Then I leave it.

Sometimes, of course, because I'm human and weak, I find myself fretting again. I've snatched the problem back. As Seinfeld would say, I "re-fret." What to do? Give it back to the Lord, of course.

Repeat as necessary.

CREATE IN ME A CLEAN HEART, O GOD, AND RENEW A STEADFAST SPIRIT WITHIN ME. (Psalm 51:10)

"There are two sides to every story." A smug cliché with a destructive effect. It seeks to make everyone comfortable by minimizing sin or wrongdoing. There are no people who destroy relationships, just people who grow apart. There is no one who sins, only those who make mistakes.

Wake up.

The fact is that people indeed sin against other people all the time. There's an incredible amount of selfishness in us and around us. If every story has two sides, all too often there's a right side and a wrong side.

As a disciple of Jesus Christ you have a responsibility to see sin and selfishness for what they are and to help and support those who have been wronged. It is not acceptable to justify what a selfish person did. Giving such support, however, may mean extending your neck a little.

HOW LONG, O LORD, WILL I CALL FOR HELP, AND THOU WILT NOT HEAR? (Habakkuk 1:2)

"The opera ain't over 'til the fat lady sings." I don't know who first said this or when, but it's a prosaic way of expressing a theme that runs through both testaments.

Habakkuk is one of my favorite books in the Old Testament. He watches all the evil around him in pre-exile Judah and urgently begs God to reveal why He allows it. In brief, God's reply is that He isn't finished yet.

This is really all we need to grasp the concept of the sovereignty of God. All is not lost. It is not hopeless. No matter how out of control the world may seem, it isn't over until God says it is.

In the meantime, we follow Him.

.

BEFORE THEY HEAR I WILL ANSWER, WHILE THEY ARE YET SPEAKING I WILL HEAR. (Isaiah 65:24 RSV)

If I am feeling pain, I'm stuck with the moment. I can't go back to yesterday or skip ahead to a better day. My thinking is limited to time as I know it.

Sometimes, when I'm puzzling over God's ways and reasons, when I think I'm seeing only inaction from God, it helps me to remember that He is not trapped in time. When I think about the marvel of being able to hear someone before he or she speaks, I may feel a little confused or even irritated at my inability to understand. I am also oddly comforted.

Learn to rejoice in the Lord's unsearchable ways instead of trying to second guess them.

OH GOD, SHATTER THEIR TEETH IN THEIR MOUTH; (Psalm 58:6)

This prayer that David uttered is a little shocking. The hundred-dollar word for such a prayer is *imprecatory*. We may wonder if there's a place for imprecatory prayer under the New Covenant.

We've probably all wanted to pray such a prayer when someone has hurt us badly or we feel threatened, but we dismiss the thought as sinful. It's not politically correct somehow.

How could David say such a thing so boldly? Probably because his motives were pure. True, he prayed for his own personal situations (Psalm 59); but when you read the whole psalm and get the total picture, it's clear he wants God to triumph. He is interested in the glory of God for God's sake, not his own.

It's all about motives. God sees through them.

BUT AS FOR ME, I SHALL WALK IN MY INTEGRITY
(Psalm 26:11)

Most secrets are evil. Even when they are meant for some imagined good, the results are usually misunderstanding and damaged relationships.

When we manipulate to get desired results, those who have been manipulated will eventually feel hurt or even betrayed. A wall of mistrust will go up and may never come down.

Secrets may seem harmless, but they almost never are.

HE SWEARS TO HIS OWN HURT AND DOES NOT CHANGE (Psalm 15:4)

This psalm defines a person of integrity succinctly. Personal integrity is a terribly important trait for a Christian. Non-Christians are quick to notice lapses of integrity in professed Christians because they hold us to a higher standard. We must have personal integrity.

The psalm deals with several indispensable pieces of integrity, but I'm focusing on one especially, that of keeping our word. We are to keep promises we've made even when it may harm us in some way.

You know how disappointing it is when someone breaks a promise to you, but how many times have you broken promises yourself? Don't make promises lightly. You may forget the promise. The person you made the promise to may even forget. The Lord will remember.

He doesn't condone broken promises.

THE LORD IS NEAR TO THE BROKENHEARTED, AND SAVES THOSE WHO ARE CRUSHED IN SPIRIT.
(Psalm 34:18)

How important this verse is at painful times in our lives. It is also a verse you can claim for someone else who is grieving or feeling hopeless.

Sometimes people hit bottom through no fault of their own. The situation may have been caused by someone else. Sometimes they hit bottom because they are living out the consequences of choices they have made.

It takes time to figure it out. Sometimes repentance, a turning away from past patterns, is necessary. Sometimes, as with Job, endurance and trust are the only alternatives. Whatever the situation, this promise is here.

I WILL INSTRUCT YOU AND TEACH YOU IN THE WAY WHICH YOU SHOULD GO (Psalm 32:8)

Consistent time spent reading scripture and in prayer are the lifeblood of a Christian walk. This isn't a newsflash. It has been stressed so many times, we almost don't hear it after a while.

Once we've accepted that, we usually look for structure and guidance from a daily devotional. I am giving you three recommendations: Oswald Chambers, Oswald Chambers, and Oswald Chambers.

He is not easy. He is as relentless and challenging as your Christian walk is. He is frustrating at times because he refuses to focus on anything except Jesus Christ, and there is no nonsense or sentiment. No excuses.

I know a woman who tore up his book one day and then bought another one.

AND HIS MASTER PRAISED THE UNJUST STEWARD BECAUSE HE ACTED SHREWDLY; FOR THE SONS OF THIS AGE ARE MORE SHREWD IN RELATION TO THEIR OWN KIND THAN THE SONS OF LIGHT.

(Luke 16:8)

The parable of the unjust steward is befuddling. Sometimes the more subtle meanings in the parables will become clear only when explained by experts who understand the ways of the Middle East. However, even without going into that here, one thing is clear.

The man was a rascal. He was a sinner. But he knew his master. He knew that this particular master would admire his resourcefulness and would grant mercy based on that.

Jesus is saying that the people of the world understand each other better than the people of God understand each other or their Master.

If we seek the Lord's face fervently and often, we will no longer have to ask Him what His will is. We will know it because we know Him.

WHEN JESUS SAW HIM AND KNEW THAT HE HAD BEEN LYING THERE A LONG TIME, HE SAID TO HIM, "DO YOU WANT TO BE HEALED?" (John 5:6)

I often struggle with anger. It's anger and hurt I've let accumulate for many years. Naturally I feel totally justified. Don't we always?

I could go to a counselor who may even tell me I'm right. Whether judging me wrong or right, the counselor will certainly understand when I say something trendy like, "I don't know what to do with all my anger."

The truth is I do know what to do with it. Jesus has already taught me that. The outcome depends on whether I truly want to be healed.

He asked a penetrating question.

BUT MARY TREASURED UP ALL THESE THINGS, PONDERING THEM IN HER HEART. (Luke 2:19)

I heard someone say that once you have a child, you will live the rest of your life with your heart walking around outside your own body.

Handling such total vulnerability is difficult. We become protective and defensive. We may give lip service to wanting our child to be a Christian. We may say we want to see strength and courage. At the core of it, though, what our emotions really want for that child is security and happiness. And we want it all the time.

Mary must have felt intense pain and helplessness. There had to be times when she felt alienated and shut out by her son; but look at her with new eyes by reading about the miracle at Cana when Jesus turned the water into wine.

She was strong enough to insist that He do it and wise enough to place her full confidence in Him. If she knew He could do that, she was also placing her confidence in God's plan. She said to the servants, "Whatever He says to you, do it."

Those are her last recorded words in the scriptures, and there could not be a better model for our discipleship. Take Mary's advice.

AND JESUS ANSWERED AND SAID, "WERE THERE NOT TEN CLEANSED? BUT THE NINE, WHERE ARE THEY?" (Luke 17:17)

We all know the story of Jesus' healing of the ten lepers. Only one returned to give thanks.

Usually we dwell on the lesson of gratitude. We need to look in our own hearts and express thanks. Even if we don't always live this out, we get the point.

There's a second perspective on this story, though. It's looking at it from Jesus' vantage point. He was the one putting out all the energy and getting very little in return for it.

Sometimes you will be the one who is doing that. This story is a reality check. Reality is that the thankfulness return for many of your best efforts will be very small. That's the way it is.

Jesus didn't tell his disciples to stop doing good because no one appreciated it. He wasted no time moaning about what *should* be. He blessed the one who showed appreciation and dropped it.

We must do that too.

HE HAS DUG A PIT AND HOLLOWED IT OUT, AND HAS FALLEN INTO THE HOLE WHICH HE MADE.
(Psalm 7:15)

The Golden Rule is about grace. So is the practice of giving someone more rope.

How many times in the past have you been the recipient of God's grace? Being born in comfortable circumstances instead of miserable poverty? Driving drunk and somehow making it home safely without hurting anybody else? Taking unfair advantage of someone else? Stubbornly refusing to forgive someone? Ignoring God's call somehow, putting it off to answer later?

For myself, I'm ashamed to say all of the above are true. God chose to extend grace to me over and over again. Would I still be getting more rope if I had continued to ignore and rebel? Maybe. And then again, maybe not. I don't know.

Be aware that He is extending grace to you now. Every day. You have been kept from falling into the hole.

IF YOU DO NOT FORGIVE MEN, THEN YOUR FATHER WILL NOT FORGIVE YOUR TRANSGRESSIONS. (Matthew 6:15)

"I can forgive, but I can't forget." This may sound reasonable, but most of the time it is self-righteous and foolish.

Forgiving is not optional for disciples of Christ. It is a command. Jesus told us to do it. He did not say, "Forgive when you feel like it." Therefore, it must be possible to do it even when we don't feel it.

Sometimes we think we don't know how to do it.

The forgiveness part is an act of will. It is not an emotion. Simply ask God for the will to forgive and be rid of it. Give it up.

The forgetting will follow, maybe slowly. Forgetting is not amnesia, and it's not repressing or refusing to confront the hurt. You'll know you have forgotten when you realize one day that you're no longer torn apart by the pain, and the pain no longer determines your actions. You may never reach the point where you can recall the hurt totally without emotion, but it will no longer have the power to take your mind into bad places.

AND HE CAME TO THE DISCIPLES AND FOUND THEM SLEEPING. (Matthew 26:40)

"Just preach to us the simple gospel." Many Christians love to say that. Mostly, I hear them say it when they've listened to a message that made them uncomfortable or angry, a message urging them to do something.

Okay. Here are some simple gospels:

Blessed are the peacemakers, for they shall be called sons of God. (Matthew 5:9)

For whoever wishes to save his life shall lose it; but whoever loses his life for My sake and the gospel's shall save it. (Mark 8:35)

And why do you call me "Lord, Lord," and do not do what I say? (Luke 6:46)

This I command you, that you love one another. (John 15:17)

How simple is it?

EACH MAN'S WORK WILL BECOME EVIDENT: FOR THE DAY WILL SHOW IT, BECAUSE IT IS TO BE REVEALED WITH FIRE; AND THE FIRE ITSELF WILL REVEAL THE QUALITY OF EACH MAN'S WORK.

(I Corinthians 3:12)

What things are eternal?

We understand obsolescence. We expect nearly everything to fall apart or become outmoded, even marriages and great ideas.

Think about your own life. What have you spent your time and energy on that will survive the fire? What should you spend your time on?

Your list will be short.

MY MIND INSTRUCTS ME IN THE NIGHT.
(Psalm 16:7)

Great Grandma Lindback was often awake for long periods every night. As a child, I had no empathy. Why in the world couldn't she just go to bed and sleep?

Now I have night journeys along three different paths. Sometimes I allow myself to be led by the dark forces. This path takes me from gloom to despair to paranoia.

Sometimes I put myself on prayer duty, wondering who needs my prayers at that specific time but knowing I don't need to know.

The third path is nearly as agitating as the first. My mind may suddenly open up to receive insights, guidance, motivation, instructions. Sometimes peace follows. Sometimes not.

I understand Grandma better now.

ALL SCRIPTURE IS INSPIRED BY GOD AND PROFITABLE FOR TEACHING, FOR REPROOF, FOR CORRECTION, FOR TRAINING IN RIGHTEOUSNESS.
(2 Timothy: 3:16)

The inerrancy of scripture is an emotional issue. It divides believers. You may feel pressure to decide what you think because it's important to some people that sides be taken.

Jesus used parables. Nobody expects or needs them to be historical fact. Rigidity on this subject may display small faith, not great faith.

God has accomplished many things through imperfect people who have been led by Him to do His work, and that includes the imperfect, faithful, Spirit-inspired people He used to write His message to us.

There was only one task that required perfection. For that He sent His Son.

GUARD, THROUGH THE HOLY SPIRIT WHO DWELLS IN US, THE TREASURE WHICH HAS BEEN ENTRUSTED TO YOU. (2 Timothy 1:14)

Many Christians make fun of intellectuals and scholars. "I don't need all that education to be a Christian."

Scripture is a treasure entrusted to us. We should be thanking God for providing Bible scholars and language experts down through the centuries to guard the integrity of the writing. If you've ever played the childhood "telephone" game, where a whispered message is passed from person to person around a room, you get the point. Human nature embellishes, distorts, and just plain gets things wrong.

It's the scribes, monks, and nitpickers who have kept the message the same down through all the centuries. The Dead Sea Scrolls, not found until the 1940s, showed almost no variations. What an excellent job they have done.

AND JESUS, FULL OF THE HOLY SPIRIT, RETURNED FROM THE JORDAN AND WAS LED ABOUT BY THE SPIRIT IN THE WILDERNESS FOR FORTY DAYS, BEING TEMPTED BY THE DEVIL. (Luke 4:1)

We should not overlook or trivialize the forty days Jesus spent in the wilderness, being tempted by Satan. It was not easy just because He was Jesus.

It must have been a miserable ordeal, all the more so because He knew exactly what lay ahead of Him if He chose to do the job. He was planning. Whether Satan literally transported Him is unimportant. It was a heinous spiritual struggle.

Satan threw in front of Him every possible way of making the mission easier. He suggested compromise, manipulating people with the spectacular, shortcuts, gimmicks, and abuse of God's power. It is hard to hold back from using power when we have it.

Jesus anchored Himself with scripture and somehow came out with His ministry and purpose clear in His mind and the path decided. He had chosen the difficult way.

REPENT, FOR THE KINGDOM OF HEAVEN IS AT HAND. (Matthew 4:17)

"It's a jungle out there." Jesus told us that Satan is the ruler of this world. We don't have as many details about it as we would like, but we accept it because Jesus said it was so.

In the book of Matthew, Jesus talks quite a bit about God's kingdom. He speaks of living in the kingdom while we are still here on earth, not just of what the kingdom in heaven will be like.

The kingdom on earth is separate from the world, but it's probably more like an arbor than a protective bubble. While we live in this jungle, overgrown with danger and evil, we are to draw others into the arbor with us.

The evil surrounds us. We are not sealed off from it, and we are not excused from confronting it. We are to invite others into the arbor. We are to love and help others whether they are under the arbor or outside. We don't have to conquer the jungle.

DO NOT WITHHOLD GOOD FROM THOSE TO WHOM IT IS DUE, WHEN IT IS IN YOUR POWER TO DO IT. (Proverbs 3:27)

"Come on over sometime. Anytime." I've been a newcomer many times, and I have learned that an open-ended, vague invitation like that is not a gesture of friendship. It's nothing.

Another poor choice is "Our (fill-in-the-blank) group meets every Thursday. Why don't you come?"

A genuine effort to befriend someone or ease the way into a new situation means making your effort one-to-one first. When you invite someone to get together at a specific time, you are doing something meaningful. You are offering yourself.

If you haven't offered a piece of your time to that person, you haven't done anything.

HE WHO SUPPLIES SEED TO THE SOWER AND
BREAD FOR FOOD WILL SUPPLY AND MULTIPLY
YOUR SEED FOR SOWING AND INCREASE THE
HARVEST OF YOUR RIGHTEOUSNESS.

(2 Corinthians 9:10)

Trying to remain open to spiritual growth and still stand steadfast in faith can be a dilemma sometimes. The world is very confusing and seductive, but there's a kind of Christianity that is rigid and afraid of new ideas and insights. I've known weeks at a time of frustration, feeling almost torn apart by conflicting ideas. I've even asked, "Is this Satan trying to lure me off course, or is it You, Lord, trying to change my old idea and show me something better?"

Oswald Chambers offered the best help when he pointed out in *My Utmost for His Highest* that I can't think a spiritual muddle clear; I must obey it clear.

Pray for an obedient heart and the open mind mentioned in the twenty-fourth chapter of Luke. The muddles will clear as you carefully work your way along.

IF YOU ABIDE IN MY WORD, THEN YOU ARE TRULY DISCIPLES OF MINE; AND YOU SHALL KNOW THE TRUTH, AND THE TRUTH SHALL MAKE YOU FREE. (John 8: 31-32)

"The truth hurts, doesn't it?" Wrong.

The truth may annoy. It may agitate, but ultimately it cannot hurt. While leading into some difficult places, it can only bring enlightenment and better spiritual health.

Ben Bradlee, when he was editor of the *Washington Post*, is said to have ordered his reporters to stop being so concerned with finding the truth and just to get the facts. He knew that the truth would emerge as the facts piled up. It was undoubtedly good journalism, and there's spiritual wisdom there too.

Truth is the big picture. If we don't shrink from it, even in seemingly painful areas of our personal lives, we will always come to growth and healing. Satan controls repression and rationalization. All truth rests with God.

FOR THE WEAPONS OF OUR WARFARE ARE NOT OF THE FLESH, BUT DIVINELY POWERFUL FOR THE DESTRUCTION OF FORTRESSES. (2 Corinthians 10:4)

The fourth and fifth verses of 2 Corinthians 10 describe perfectly what has happened in the mind of someone who has turned away from God. Jesus spoke very plainly about the presence and influence of Satan and the spiritual battles going on all around us. The battles are vicious and real, and they're happening right now.

If you are concerned about someone who seems to be fighting or rejecting God, or worse yet, is indifferent, you can make this scripture passage part of your prayers. Ask God to employ spiritual weapons to break down the barriers that have been built up in that person's mind.

Prayer is a spiritual weapon. It is not a last resort or the wimpiest thing you can do. It is the most powerful thing you can do.

THEN JEREMIAH TOOK ANOTHER SCROLL AND GAVE IT TO BARUCH . . . AND HE WROTE ON IT AT THE DICTATION OF JEREMIAH ALL THE WORDS OF THE BOOK WHICH JEHOIAKIM KING OF JUDAH HAD BURNED IN THE FIRE; AND MANY SIMILAR WORDS WERE ADDED TO THEM. (Jeremiah 36:32)

I greatly admire the prophet Jeremiah. He is a fascinating study of loyalty, obedience, and humility; but what I respect the most about him is that he persevered in spite of constant failure. He worked so hard to turn the people of Jerusalem around before it was too late, but they did not turn.

Still, Jeremiah kept on. He was totally focused. He concerned himself only with obedience to God.

I think it was Edmund Burke who said, "Never despair, but if you do, work on in despair." Jeremiah did that.

We should all be so obedient.

IN THE BEGINNING GOD CREATED THE HEAVENS AND THE EARTH. (Genesis 1:1)

Genesis is controversial and, in many ways, cannot be explained away. You will hear some say that Moses wrote it. Others will say is was J and E and P. Some will say every word is literally true. Others will say it is a myth, an allegory, or a parable. Some will say none of it has any truth, factually or symbolically.

None of that bothers me, and it shouldn't trouble you. Jesus used parables. The truths and principles are in them, and we're responsible for living by those principles. God reveals many basic truths about how He thinks and operates in the book of Genesis, and we're responsible for understanding and living those too.

God owns the truth. You don't need to fear the truth or discussions about it.

NOW THE SERPENT WAS MORE CRAFTY THAN ANY BEAST OF THE FIELD WHICH THE LORD GOD HAD MADE. (Genesis 3:1)

Jesus consistently acknowledged the presence of Satan in this world. He called him the ruler of this world (John 12:31). I suggest going back to the early chapters of Genesis. This is a help when we try to understand what Jesus meant in the book of Matthew when he talked about the kingdom on earth.

In the first chapter of Genesis (1:2), the Holy Spirit hovers over the water. The ancient Hebrew concept of hell was swirling black water, chaos, not fire. Satan was already there. God moved in on Satan, not the other way around. The establishment of God's kingdom on earth had begun, and the last chapter is not played out yet.

WISDOM ALONG WITH AN INHERITANCE IS GOOD. (Ecclesiastes 7:11)

Cartoon: Claude's mother to teacher: "You must never be harsh with Claude. He's so sensitive. If he does misbehave, just strike the child sitting next to him. That will frighten Claude."

Try to look realistically at the nature of the world for your children. You must prepare them to live in it.

Don't run to the school to complain and "fix" every piece of unfairness you think you see. Teachers are not perfect, but the world is full of inept, unreasonable, explosive people who will become employers and supervisors. Your child may very well end up working for some of them. He or she won't have you running interference then.

If you protect your child from having any bad experiences, the child will have no experience.

BE SHREWD AS SERPENTS AND INNOCENT AS DOVES. (Matthew 10:16)

When I was a child, it was popular to say that children should be seen and not heard. It's been forty years since I heard anyone say that. Now what I hear quite often is "My children come first." Is that any better?

I'm always impressed when writers refer to the Greek philosophers, so I think I should too. My grasp of philosophy is feeble, but I think it was Aristotle who taught that a virtue lies in the center between its two extremes.

Mouthy, demanding children seem to surround us. When we boast that our children always come first, we are not being good parents. We are teaching them to put their own wants ahead of others' needs. How can this be a good thing?

Your children need to see you put others ahead of them from time to time, and they need to understand why.

FOR I HAVE BEEN INFORMED CONCERNING YOU, MY BRETHREN. . . . THAT THERE ARE QUARRELS AMONG YOU. (1 Corinthians 1:11)

My younger brother John was a gentle, happy child. Since he almost never showed ill temper, our whole neighborhood was shocked when he bit his little friend Matthew. The news spread quickly. My parents were aghast.

"Why?" we all cried. "Why would you do such a thing to Matthew?"

"Because he said God didn't make ants."

Deep inside most of us are beliefs we can't bear to have challenged. When this happens within the church family, we become emotional and behave badly. We would probably bite too if we dared.

This is a major problem among believers and leads to many broken relationships. A mature Christian controls such emotions when hit with opposition. Grace, grace, grace.

IT IS FINISHED. (John 19:30)

Endings are hard. There are many reasons. Sometimes we don't want something to end because we found it to be good. Sometimes we feel awkward and miserable because it was not good, and we're not satisfied leaving it that way. Sometimes we have no control over the ending. It was someone else's choice and very painful. Or it may be that we just don't know how to bring something to an end.

Jesus always knew when to quit. He knew when hearts were too hard to listen to Him. He knew when He needed to get away and spend time alone. He knew when to end his ministry and give Himself up to the authorities.

On the cross, even though the world was still full of people who wanted His help and healing, He could say, "It is finished." We need to pray for help with this in our own lives.

Pray for the ability to see when it's time to move on and for the strength to follow through.

SO THE LORD SAID TO JOSHUA, "RISE UP! WHY IS IT THAT YOU HAVE FALLEN ON YOUR FACE!"
(Joshua 7:10)

Beginnings are hard: finding the first sentence for a letter or an apology, moving to a new place, starting a new project.

We usually think of a beginning as happening before an ending. Just as often, though, a beginning must happen after something has ended. At such times we may feel broken or defeated, and the last thing we want to do is start again. These beginnings are the most difficult.

God told both Elijah (1 Kings 19:15) and Joshua to get up and start over. There was still work for both of them. It's inevitable that God will be telling you the same thing more than once in your life.

The author was born in northern Minnesota in 1943. Her life was quite ordinary until 1976 when Bud McCulloch entered it. He was raising his seven children by himself. She added her six-year-old son to the mix and took on the challenge. They now have a home in Cass County, Minnesota, and spend time doing various kinds of mission/volunteer work.